Featuring:

Rowena Cade (1893-1983) ~ *who built the magnificent Minack Theatre on a cliff top in Cornwall.*

Margaret Mee (1909-1988) ~ *the botanical artist and Amazon adventurer.*

David Munrow (1942-1976) ~ *a pioneer in the exploration of medieval music, and a collector of exotic instruments.*

Manfred Eicher (b. 1943) ~ *the founder of ECM, one of the world's most imaginative record labels.*

Margaret Ramsay (1908-1991) ~ *a powerful force in the world of theatre, who championed new works and new writers.*

Kenji Ogawa (b. 1949) ~ *an internationally recognised ice sculptor based in Sydney, whose works promote humanitarian causes.*

Olegas Truchanas (1923-1972) ~ *photographer, explorer and defender of Tasmanian wilderness.*

Published by
Ice Calm Pty Ltd,
Sydney.

ISBN 0 9578508 0 8

Printed and bound by
McPherson's Printing.

Motivation / Biography

SEVEN EXTRAORDINARY PEOPLE

Seven inspirational lives
Seven unique achievements

Compiled by Paul Saintilan

PREFACE

This book celebrates the lives of seven
people who share the following attributes:

- They are unique, extraordinary personalities,
  rich in imagination and adventure;

- They are all twentieth century figures who
  have achieved some recognition, but not
  widespread fame;

- They have not been primarily motivated by
  money or fame, but by an artistic mission
  they set for themselves;

- They have devoted themselves to their cause
  with passion and persistence for at least a
  decade, and in most cases several decades;

- They have all left behind a creative
  achievement of great beauty as their legacy.

ROWENA CADE
(1893-1983)

Rowena Cade dreamt of, and built with her own hands, the magnificent Minack Theatre in Cornwall. This 750 seat theatre is carved into the side of a granite cliff face, in the style of an ancient Roman amphitheatre, overlooking the rugged Cornish coastline. It lies at the western end of Porthcurno beach, seven miles south-west of Penzance. For over fifty years she poured her labour, money and inspiration into the project. Today, audiences congregate each summer for a seventeen week season of performances, featuring works such as Shakespeare's The Tempest, *or Gilbert & Sullivan's* The Pirates of Penzance. *From your seat on the cliff top, you can gaze down on the turquoise water below, and out to the panorama of Logan Rock and the Atlantic Ocean.*

Rowena Cade was born on the 2nd of August 1893 in Spondon, Derbyshire. The second of four children, she spent a comfortable and carefree childhood in "The Homestead", an impressive three-story mansion not far from her father's cotton mill.

On her father's retirement in 1906 the family moved to Cheltenham, living a lifestyle of Victorian gentility until the arrival of the First World War. She then found work in the stables of Sir John Gilbey's estate at Elsenham, where she selected and broke horses for the front lines. Her accommodation at Elsenham was an old shepherd's caravan, a small wooden wagon that would not have looked misplaced on the prairies of the American Wild West.

At the conclusion of the War, with her father dead and her immediate family dispersed as far as Australia, they sold the house in Cheltenham. Sometime later Rowena and her mother rented a house at Lamorna near the Minack headland on the Western tip of Cornwall, not far from Land's End. The dark, rocky coastline ('Minack' means a 'rocky place' in Cornish), the beautiful turquoise water, the gulls and cormorants, the Cornish stories of fishermen, smugglers and shipwrecks, must have all combined to captivate her, and she bought the headland above Minack Rock for £100.

She had a house built for her and her mother on the land, using granite cut from a local quarry. West Cornwall in the twenties was quite isolated, and entertainment tended to be self-made out of sheer necessity. Several amateur theatrical productions were mounted at the Minack House and its garden, and she discovered a talent for designing and making props and costumes.

In 1928 she and her friends staged *A Midsummer Night's Dream* in a meadow at nearby Crean. When someone proposed *The Tempest* as the next venture, the Cade's garden on the headland sprang to mind as an ideal location. However seating an audience would have presented a problem. One day she looked at the gully of gorse and heather directly above Minack Rock, and wondered whether a stage and seating could be fashioned into the contours of the gully. She then set about to build it, at the age of 38, commencing a project that would consume the next fifty years of her life.

In the harsh winter of 1931-32, she and two local men, Billy Rawlings (her gardener) and Thomas Angove, spent six months building a simple stage and some rough seating. She apprenticed herself to the two men, learning how to cut granite by hand from surrounding boulders, and to inch the stones into place.

The first performance of *The Tempest* in the summer of 1932 was a triumph, and received a write-up in *The Times*. The magic of the location, with the set bathed in moonlight and surrounded by a silver sea, served to enhance the experience rather than distract the audience from the play. Improvements to the Theatre continued for the next seven years, until World War II intervened. The threat of invasion saw barbed wire lace its way around the headland, defences which she regularly overcame to cut the grass. During this time she acted as a billeting officer for children who had been evacuated to escape the Blitz. In 1944, a film crew descended on the Theatre to shoot *Love Story*, a Gainsborough film starring Stewart Grainger and Margaret Lockwood. Props included a grand piano, but filming was interrupted by savage weather, and the production retreated to the safety of a studio.

When the War was over, most of the enhancements of the mid-thirties had deteriorated, reducing the site to the basic structure of 1932. She worked hard to rebuild what had been lost, and ever resourceful, converted a World War II gun post into the Theatre's Box Office. In the post war period, as the Theatre's reputation spread, it became clear that the Theatre itself needed to be separated from her private garden. In the early fifties she and Billy Rawlings completed this work, which included granite walls, an access road, a car park, and a flight of ninety steps up from the beach.

Unable to afford granite for the seating, she developed a technique for working with cement.

The cement seats in the Theatre are engraved with the names of past productions (such as 'Hamlet 1962', 'The Taming of the Shrew 1960'), and intricate Celtic designs, decorations which Rowena supplied with the tip of an old screwdriver before the cement dried. When Billy Rawlings died in 1966, she inscribed the one granite seat in the Theatre as his memorial.

Despite her slender physique, Rowena never shirked the hard physical work, and carried sand from Porthcurno beach up to the site on her back, and on one occasion, fifteen foot beams of driftwood from a wrecked freighter. She worked on the Theatre each winter in all conditions until she was in her mid-eighties. There is a photo of her aged 85 sitting in an upturned wheelbarrow next to the Theatre reading a book.

Around this time, in 1976, she gave the Minack Theatre to a Charitable Trust which was established to plan for its future, and ensure it long outlived her. In all her years devoted to the Theatre it had never been profitable. Each short season had never generated sufficient income to cover the running costs and construction work, and she personally funded the annual shortfall. The new Trust extended the summer season, built an Exhibition Centre with an admission fee, enlarged the retailing operation, and undertook other activities which drew a bigger audience and made the Theatre financially viable for the first time. To this day it is self-supporting, receiving not one penny in subsidy from local or national government departments.

Each summer's seventeen week season, from mid May to mid September, provides seventeen amateur theatre companies one week each to present a production. This ensures constant variety and reasonable ticket prices. In any given week there are around five evening performances and two matinées. Since *The Tempest* was first performed in 1932, Shakespeare has been central to the Minack's programming. Gilbert & Sullivan has also been hugely successful, particularly *The Pirates of Penzance*, a perennial favourite. Other types of entertainment have been tried, including comedy, opera, ballet, concert, son et lumière and male voice choir. Even out of season, to wander down the Minack Theatre's myriad paths and byways, gazing out onto the spectacular views, is an inspirational experience.

Further reading: www.minack.com

The Minack Theatre, Porthcurno, Penzance, Cornwall, TR19 6JU, UK.

MARGARET MEE
(1909-1988)

Margaret Mee was a botanical artist and adventurer, who devoted over thirty years of her life to recording the threatened flora of the Amazonian rainforests. A delicate, feminine woman, Mrs Mee would pack a .32 Rossi revolver with her sketch pad, brushes and watercolours, and head up the Amazon in her canoe, accompanied by a local boatman, braving snakes, spiders and cannibals in the pursuit of rare species. Her paintings record in exquisite detail the identifying characteristics of many rare (and in some cases now extinct) tropical plant species.

Margaret Hendersen Brown was born at
Chesham, Buckinghamshire, in 1909. Her
independent personality and passionate embrace
of political causes were evident from a young
age. At the first opportunity she left her family
and moved by herself to London, where she met
Reg Bartlett, a Trade Union member to whom
she was briefly married. Even among her
communist friends she stood out, being known
as the only woman who would turn up to
demonstrations in high heels and make-up.
During the thirties she devoted herself to working
with the under-privileged, and attacking the
Fascist movement in Britain and Spain.

Having studied art as a girl, she served as a
draughtsman in an aircraft factory during World
War II, and afterwards studied at the Camberwell
School of Art, and then at St. Martin's, where she
met her second husband, Greville Mee, a
commercial artist.

In 1952 she and her new husband moved to
Brazil, to care for her ailing sister. During this
time she taught art in São Paulo's British School,

and began her first tentative ventures into the wild, exploring the coastal rainforests around the São Paulo area where they lived. She found numerous botanical subjects, and sketched them with accuracy and sensitivity.

Her great Amazon adventure began in 1956 at the age of 47, when she visited the Gurupi River. In 1960 she was invited to participate in a project called 'Flora Brasilica', to supply illustrations for a reference book on bromeliads. Even in the age of photography, botanical art is important for naturalists, as it vividly depicts the identifying characteristics of a species, in ways that are difficult for photography. She spent five years travelling around north-east Brazil researching the project, becoming an expert on the bromeliad family in the process. She eventually discovered a number of new species in the Amazon forests - three of which are named after her.

In 1967 she exhibited her work at London's Tryon Gallery, to promote the publication of a folio edition of *Flowers of the Brazilian Forests*. This edition of 32 plates was created with the support of Prince Philip, and received widespread acclaim.

She was captivated by the beauty of exotic flowers, waxing lyrical about the colouring of the blue orchid, or the intense perfume of the Amazon Moonflower. It took her some years to fulfil her ambition of painting the Moonflower, as it only flowers on one evening a year, under a full moon.

The deforestation of Brazil during the 1960s, 70s and 80s was a source of considerable anguish to her. The pristine rainforest that she had encountered when she first ventured up the Amazon River and its tributaries was slowly ravaged, some areas such as the Rio Negro experiencing wholesale destruction. While she always had the dual motivation to discover plants that were unknown, and to record plants before they were wiped out, it was the latter that appeared to dominate her thinking in later years. She began to campaign for the conservation of the Brazilian jungle, and also voiced concerns over the welfare of the forest Indians.

Margaret Mee made fifteen journeys into the Amazonian rainforest over a thirty year period. During her travels she survived bouts of malaria and hepatitis, frequent dangers from insects and reptiles, and on one occasion was forced to draw her revolver to repel the advances of a drunken gold prospector. Her last Amazon expedition took place in May 1988 at the age of 79. Returning to the 'safety' of civilisation, she was killed in a car accident in the English Midlands.

The Margaret Mee Amazon Trust was established in the year of her death to draw attention to Brazil's ecological crisis.

Further reading:
The Daily Telegraph Book of Obituaries
ed. Hugh Massingberd, Pan Books, 1996

DAVID MUNROW
(1942-1976)

David Munrow was a pioneer in the exploration of medieval and renaissance music. He dragged the music out of its scholarly confines and blew away the dust and cobwebs with energetic, exuberant performances. He collected exotic instruments, from Bolivian flutes to replicas of long lost antiquities that had to be specially crafted through reference to old manuscripts. He offended some early music specialists, who considered him at times unscholarly. But no one doubted that his performances brought the music to life, and he was recognised as the first great populariser of 'early music'. He tragically took his own life in 1976, bringing his career to a premature close at the age of 34.

David Munrow was born in 1942, and first demonstrated his passion for exotic musical instruments in 1960 at the age of 18, while teaching in Peru under the British Council Overseas Voluntary Scheme. He returned from South America with Bolivian flutes, Peruvian pipes, and dozens of other obscure instruments. The following year at Cambridge he saw a crumhorn hanging on a wall in a friend's study, which directed his attention towards medieval and renaissance music.

After finishing his studies at Cambridge he spent a year researching seventeenth century bawdy songs at Birmingham University. He then landed a job playing bassoon and recorder for the Royal Shakespeare Theatre in Stratford, adding more obscure instruments from Shakespeare's era to his repertoire as time progressed. This period provided an opportunity for him to research renaissance and medieval instruments, through intensive reading and experimentation.

In 1967 he became a lecturer in early music history at Leicester University, and in the same year formed the Early Music Consort of London, with James Bowman, Oliver Brookes, and Christopher Hogwood (James Tyler joined in 1969). The Consort won a large and devoted following through its slick and thrilling performances of medieval and renaissance music. He liked to immerse himself in every aspect of recording an album or presenting a concert, and his skill at programming became highly regarded. 1968 marked the Consort's first overseas tour, and Munrow availed himself of these opportunities to add to his collection of exotic instruments. He also commissioned craftsmen to reconstruct long lost instruments.

He claimed to experience considerable excitement waiting for the arrival of the Consort's finished records, which would be replaced by a growing dissatisfaction once he started playing them as he considered other interpretative possibilities. He disliked listening to medieval music at home, because listening to his own recordings tortured him, and he was highly critical of others, so he played folk or jazz music instead.

For Munrow, the truth lay in whether an idea worked musically *in performance*, and he was frustrated by the musical arguments in which he found himself embroiled, which he seemed to regard as dry, academic, one-upmanship.

The Consort scored a notable success at the Proms in 1969 with a performance of Dufay songs and fifteenth century basse-danses. He finally succeeded in bringing his work to a worldwide audience with the scores for the BBC TV series *The Six Wives of Henry VIII* and *Elizabeth R*. This led to him providing the music for the film of *Henry VIII*, and other films such as Ken Russell's *The Devils* and John Boorman's *Zardoz*. His popularising zeal also found expression through the publication of a book (*Instruments of the Middle Ages and Renaissance*- Oxford University Press 1976), and presenting the BBC Radio 3 programme *Pied Piper*. His radio show was not restricted to medieval music, but roamed free and wide over his diverse tastes. He collected obscure records as well as instruments, and was proud that much of what he played on air came from his private

collection, and wouldn't have been found in the
BBC library.

*Further reading: www.medieval.org;
Gramophone magazine May 1974, July 1976.*

MANFRED EICHER
(b. 1943)

*Manfred Eicher single-handedly built ECM
(Edition of Contemporary Music) into one of the
most prolific and imaginative record labels in the
world. Over a thirty year period the label has
released over 700 recordings, making a major
contribution to jazz, 'world' music, and
experimental music genres. The label has been a
home to names such as Keith Jarrett, Jan
Garbarek, Pat Metheny, Chick Corea, Arvo Pärt,
Giya Kancheli, Steve Reich and John Adams.
ECM started with the most modest resources,
and achieved its success primarily through
Eicher's artistic intuition. The label's success is
also due to its distinctive cover artwork, beautiful
packaging, transparent recording aesthetic, and
inspired programming (featuring extraordinary
juxtapositions of style and genre).*

Manfred Eicher was born in 1943, and studied at the Academy of Music in Berlin. He played classical and jazz bass, and worked as an assistant producer on chamber music recordings. His poetic nature took to heart the respect for nuance and subtlety that lies at the centre of classical sound recording, and he endeavoured to apply the same sensitivity to recording jazz. In 1969 he founded the Edition of Contemporary Music (ECM), based in Munich, assuming the roles of record producer, editor, artist & repertoire director and company director.

At the time of ECM's launch, the attention of the major labels had drifted away from jazz, and he found a receptive audience when he wrote to the musicians he admired, such as Keith Jarrett and Chick Corea, inviting them to record for him.

He struck gold with Keith Jarrett, whose albums (such as the *Köln Concert*) bankrolled the label, and allowed Eicher to increase the number of new releases to more that twenty per year, each with its own unique story and experimental twist.

From the late 1970s, he began to record modern composers such as Steve Reich and John Adams. He first heard Estonian composer Arvo Pärt's music while driving across Germany and fell in love with it. The experience inspired him to create the ECM New Series for the exploration of medieval and contemporary music, which was launched in 1984 with Pärt's *Tabula Rasa*. Pärt's haunting *Passio* was another highly successful addition to the catalogue.

One of the seminal recordings of the 1990s was *Officium*, a three-way collaboration between Eicher, as artistic director and record producer, the Hilliard Ensemble, and Norwegian saxophonist Jan Garbarek (who had worked with Eicher almost since their first meeting at the Bologna Jazz Festival in 1968). In an inspired juxtaposition, Eicher contrasted the Hilliard's pure vocals in the ancient *Officium defunctorum* by Morales (and other early music works) with Garbarek's powerful saxophone improvisations. Garbarek's melodic line consistently soars over the top of the voices, and then softens, blending in beautifully with the other vocal lines.

Eicher has never been a passive producer but rather a highly creative catalyst. He prompted Keith Jarrett's successful excursion into classical music, recording Bach's *Well Tempered Clavier*, the *Goldberg Variations*, the Shostakovich *Preludes and Fugues*, and Mozart Piano Concertos. Beyond jazz and classical music, ECM's catalogue travels as far as Indian raga, Scandinavian folk song, African drumming, and Brazilian choro.

The label has never lost its almost mystically inspired attention to detail. Prior to CD, ECM sought out the highest quality vinyl, eventually using the pressing facilities of the classical label Deutsche Grammophon to ensure the best possible reproduction. Even the label's CD packaging achieves a luxury far beyond that attempted by most other companies. There have been instances where ECM has packaged a single CD with a slipcase and two booklets, which would give the accountants in the major labels a heart attack.

Eicher has also contributed music to films by directors such as Jean-Luc Godard, and in 1991 co-directed his first feature film, *Holozän*, which was awarded the Special Jury Prize at the 45th Locarno Film Festival.

Further reading: www.ecmrecords.com

MARGARET RAMSAY
(1908-1991)

Margaret ("Peggy") Ramsay was a dynamic force in the theatrical world, championing new and unconventional plays in her role as agent, many works going on to become classics of twentieth century theatre and cinema.

She was a passionate advocate and creative sounding board for well known writers such as: Robert Bolt, Alan Ayckbourn, John Mortimer, Edward Bond, Willy Russell, Stephen Poliakoff, Eugène Ionesco and Joe Orton. She played a significant role in the careers of the writers she represented, and influenced their most important works as they reacted to her robust criticism and praise.

It took nearly a decade for Peggy to reach the top of her profession, where she stayed for twenty five years.

On May 27th 1908 Margaret Francesca Venniker was born in Australia, in a small town called Molong, near the Blue Mountains west of Sydney. Her parents had arrived in the country the year before on an extended honeymoon, and in 1926, after a number of years travelling, and the intervention of the first world war, the family settled back in their native South Africa, on a family farm in Oudtshoorn.

Peggy loved the harsh beauty of the landscape (and rode on some of the farm's 10,000 ostriches), but as she grew older she developed a growing discontentment with her family, and life on the farm. At the age of 18 she went to Rhodes University in Grahamstown, where she met and subsequently married Norman Ramsay, a lecturer. He was a controversial figure, and shortly after their marriage one of his business ventures failed, which motivated him to flee to England. She also sought to escape life in South Africa, and they boarded a ship for Southampton.

Peggy was unhappy in the marriage, and after a

tempestuous period on their arrival in London, they separated. She found herself alone in a new country, and later claimed she started life in England with £10 to her name. Despite being in emotional turmoil, she was also excited by her newfound freedom.

She auditioned for the Carl Rosa Opera Company, and joined the chorus, beginning a life on the road that would last on and off for two decades. During this time she worked as both a singer and actress, accumulating experience that would later be of use to her as an agent. She must have demonstrated some talent, as she often spoke of a backstage meeting with Noël Coward, who predicted she would go on to great things. During her time on the road she started a relationship with matinée idol William Roderick, which despite its ups and downs, would last fifty years.

She demonstrated very early on an ability to quickly cut to the heart of a play through the script, to be able to visualise it in performance, to see flaws and potential immediately, and to be able to articulate her thoughts clearly and forcefully. On the strength of this talent she was invited by a number of different managements to read scripts for them, providing her view on the suitability of submissions. From there she joined the Q Theatre, providing artistic input, and was involved in the presentation of a number of new plays there in 1950 and 1951.

By this time she was in her early forties, and felt she had arrived at a professional and personal impasse. As an actress she was being offered fewer and fewer roles, and she liked little of what she was offered. She had won the confidence of a number of theatre luminaries, and in 1953 three of her supporters, Edward Sutro, and Dorothy and Campbell Christie, offered to help her set up her own agency, by providing financial support and sending work in her direction. In this role she would represent playwrights, selling their work, handling the contractual arrangements, and facilitating the payment of royalties. She had misgivings about this, believing agents to be parasites, and at first declined the offer. Finally, in the autumn of 1953 at the age of 45, she agreed to give it a try.

Her main motivation was not to become an administrative clearing house, but to become intimately involved with great works and great writers, and it was into this that she channelled her considerable energy. She set up her offices at 14a Goodwin's Court, an alleyway lying off St. Martin's Lane in London's West End. She had two small offices on the first floor, in what was a converted brothel.

Through the 1950s she found life difficult, and there were two occasions when the agency came close to folding. She also had very little in the way of personal support, always maintaining a fiercely independent attitude to her private life. She found solace for her professional and personal difficulties in the writings of Beckett and Schopenhauer. She was immediately bowled over by Beckett's *Waiting for Godot*, and despite not representing him, campaigned for the play in the face of widespread disinterest.

Her passion for the works of Ionesco overstepped professional boundaries, and they had a widely discussed affair. After the shaky business start, the agency attained stability as her writers began to achieve commercial success (with major hits such as Robert Bolt's *A Man For All Seasons*, and Alan Ayckbourn's *How The Other Half Loves*).

Peggy was highly unconventional and loved to shock with her behaviour and language. She established an immediate rapport with her notorious client Joe Orton, acting as a mother figure. This role was brought to widespread attention in the film of Orton's biography *Prick Up Your Ears*. Peggy, played by Vanessa Redgrave, was the fictional narrator of the film, associating her for evermore with Orton's controversial life and death.

Peggy could infuriate people by being emotionally volatile, tyrannical, and indiscrete, but she had no equal in being able to recognise future potential and fight tooth and nail to see it realised. She dispensed her wisdom quickly and effortlessly, reading scripts as soon as she received them, and providing feedback straight away. At the height of her powers she would read at least three scripts a day. Edward Bond claimed that without her intense involvement he would have had difficulty writing his plays.

An example of her influence on a popular play is her intervention in Willy Russell's *Educating Rita*. She gave a withering critique of the first draft, complaining that the character of the tutor was too thinly realised, which not only undermined his character, but the whole potential chemistry with Rita. Although Russell felt exhausted, his efforts on the character of Rita having drained him, he knew she was right and re-wrote the play. He later said that without the re-write it would never have been successful. It not only achieved success as a play, but became a film starring Julie Walters and Michael Caine.

An attractive, feminine woman, she could be hard, unsentimental, and a fierce negotiator. When she discovered a play that she believed in, her commitment was total, and in the ensuing

fight to have it staged and recognised, she
seemed impervious to criticism. She was not
motivated by money, was repulsed by the social
dimension of theatre, rarely attending opening
nights, and scorned personal publicity, destroying
any press cuttings she found in the office that
related to her. She declined to have an entry in
Who's Who, or *Who's Who in the Theatre*.

In the 1980s Peggy's health began to decline, and
in April 1991 she suffered two blows only days
apart from which she never recovered. The first
was a fire at her offices in which precious
memorabilia was lost, and the second was the
death of Bill Roderick, her companion of fifty
years. Having largely taken him for granted, she
suddenly saw how much he had meant to her.
Her health deteriorated further, and she died on
4th September 1991 at the age of 83.

Throughout her life Peggy had acted as a creative
catalyst in bringing her writers together with
producers, publishers, directors, designers,
composers and actors. At her request, when she
died her body was cremated and the ashes

scattered in Venice's San Michèle cemetery, where Diaghilev is buried.

She left an estate worth £1.5 million (which had swelled to £3 million by 1996 when the full commission had been realised from her numerous agreements). Upon her death a trust was established called the Peggy Ramsay Foundation, which, following wishes expressed in her will, seeks to use this money to help playwrights in need of assistance, and to encourage the art of writing for the theatre.

Further reading:
Colin Chambers, Peggy: The Life of Margaret Ramsay, Play Agent.
Nick Hern Books, London, 1997.

KENJI OGAWA
(b. 1949)

Kenji Ogawa is an internationally recognised ice sculptor, whose major works promote world peace and humanitarian causes. He grew up in Japan, and served as an apprentice chef at the Hotel Okura, Tokyo, where his training included ice carving, vegetable carving, butter carving, flower display and origami. After working in Guam and Tehran, he moved to Australia in 1976 when he was appointed chef at the Japanese Consulate-General in Sydney. He became a full time ice sculptor in 1987.

In 1989 he was powerfully moved by a visit to The Great Wall of China, and returned from the trip committed to using his work as a vehicle to promote humanitarian themes. In 1990 he carved a ten tonne ice sculpture in Anchorage to mark the fall of the Berlin Wall. As a comment on the Gulf War, he transformed a fifteen metre high iceberg on Lake Portage, Alaska, into a peace symbol. He was invited to sculpt for the 50th Anniversary Celebration of the United Nations in 1995, and in 1998 created a four metre high bust of Gandhi for the Nagano Winter Olympics in Japan.

Kenji Ogawa was born in 1949 in Tokushima, Japan. His parents had been wealthy land owners in North Korea, but were forced to flee the country at the end of World War II. They were lucky to escape with their lives, and until the age of eight Kenji led an itinerant life, wandering the Japanese countryside with his family.

At high school he excelled as an athlete, and his strong, independent personality emerged. When the time came to choose a career, he was unimpressed with suggestions that his chemistry studies might qualify him for a laboratory position. He applied instead to become an apprentice chef at the prestigious Hotel Okura in Tokyo. One of the advantages he saw in such a career was that it might provide travel opportunities, and he was beginning to feel claustrophobic in Japan.

His application was successful, and despite his stay being interrupted for twelve months by illness, he completed the apprenticeship, and spent four years there. Having left his family and friends in the countryside to work in Tokyo, he had little to return home to at the end of each working day, and so he virtually lived in the kitchens, staying on long after his shift had ended, picking up pointers on cooking, ice carving and other Japanese arts.

In 1972 the management sent him to their hotel in Guam. The island at that stage was being used as a base for B52 bombers making daily raids on Vietnam. He returned to Japan in 1973, and the following year flew to Tehran, to work as a chef for the Iran Japan Petrochemical Company.

He moved to Australia in 1976 to become the chef for the Japanese Consulate-General in Sydney, which led to work at the Hilton Hotel, the Sydney Opera House and the Hotel Intercontinental. During this time he appeared on TV cooking programs demonstrating vegetable and ice carving, and won a gold medal in 1983 representing Australia at the Osaka International Gourmet Fair.

In 1986 he competed in his first ice carving championship but it became clear that the time needed to travel to international exhibitions was incompatible with holding down a hotel job, so in 1987 he left his hotel career behind to become Australia's first full-time ice sculptor. The company he established, Kenji's Ice Carving International, is now truly international: since 1987 he has exhibited in Japan, China, Alaska, Canada, the USA, New Zealand, and Norway.

In 1989 Kenji was invited to compete in a championship in the Chinese city of Harbin. He paid a visit to The Great Wall of China, and was deeply moved by the experience. From that moment he aimed to give his life a higher purpose by using his major sculptures to promote world peace and humanitarian causes. He was also impressed by the Chinese people he met on that trip, who despite lacking material wealth, seemed to possess a deep inner serenity. This held great appeal for Kenji, who is a practising Buddhist, and whose decision to follow his heart and give up his job to become an ice sculptor has meant supporting a family on reduced earnings, living simply and without material extravagance.

'Purity' of life is also important to him, and the word frequently arises in conversation. Despite being a wildly eccentric character, capable of manic energy and great fun, in 1991 after an Alaskan trip he gave up smoking and drinking "to detoxify, and become purer".

The major championships and exhibitions now pay for Kenji's participation, and he travels to Tokyo, London and New York twice a year. To survive he also undertakes corporate work for advertising and product launches. Over a three year period he carved two thousand exquisite ice fish to grace the buffet of one of Sydney's hotels, before he had to discontinue that product line, suffering from the ice sculptor's equivalent of repetitive strain injury.

The sculpture he looks back on with the fondest memories is *Celebration of Life*, his 1995 contribution to the 50th Anniversary Celebration of the United Nations. It was an ice tree encased in a 4.5 metre cocoon of ice, in the shape of a drop of water, and surrounded by ice children. The tree had five branches representing the five continents. The Canadian Government sponsored the sculpture to symbolise their work developing water purification systems, of great potential benefit to the third world. It was sculpted by Kenji and his team in a (windchill adjusted) temperature of minus 52 degrees Celsius.

His subjects include historical figures who have inspired him, such as Mahatma Gandhi and John Lennon. His bust of Gandhi at the Nagano Winter Olympics marked the fiftieth anniversary of his assassination. In October 2000 he carved the image of Lennon on the Sydney Harbour foreshores to mark what would have been Lennon's sixtieth birthday. It was also part of Kenji's 'Come Together 2000' initiative, to raise the profile of peace as an issue as the world enters a new millennium. Mother Teresa, Nelson Mandela and the Dalai Lama are three other figures he hopes to carve in the future.

For such a fragile artform, Kenji has experienced relatively few mishaps. He recounts with amusement and relief one occasion when he sculpted an ice grand piano for a party held in honour of Billy Joel. Shortly after Joel had left the function one of the ice piano legs gave way, and the whole sculpture collapsed.

His Sydney sculptures are executed in a cold room, and he employs a wide variety of tools, from the finest chisels to chainsaws. On an average commercial commission he employs twenty different implements, and needs six different types of sharpening stone to hone them to perfection. The bigger the block of ice, the fewer the tools that are required, and sculpting an iceberg requires fewer still, being largely carved by chainsaw. Power tools cut effortlessly through ice, which is a much softer material than wood, but he considers himself old fashioned, because with the exception of chainsaws he refuses to use power tools, while many younger Japanese and American ice sculptors now prefer high powered drills to chisels.

One day he was with his family at Narrabeen Lakes in Sydney, when he saw an elderly woman glide past in a kayak. That day he bought himself a kayak, and the next day a larger one for the family. He finds that kayak racing strengthens his upper body, which is advantageous for a sculptor, and his time on the river also provides quiet, serene moments of reflection, where he can revel in the beauty of water and nature.

Kenji vigorously supports a number of humanitarian causes and regularly donates his time and work to charity.

As a Buddhist, Kenji sees a purity and beauty in the process of water becoming ice, then a sculpture, and then returning back to water again, vanishing without trace into nature, leaving no waste. From the time a sculpture is completed it is constantly changing; ice sculpture is one of the great transient arts, which like a living thing blossoms and dies. Although nothing remains of his sculptures, they live on in his large collection of photos.

OLEGAS TRUCHANAS
(1923-1972)

Olegas Truchanas, the photographer and
explorer, was a passionate advocate for the
protection of Tasmania's wilderness regions. For
more than twenty years he explored Tasmania's
South-West, undertaking lone journeys into the
remotest areas, discovering major errors on
official maps, recording faithfully with his
camera scenes which he may have been the first
to witness. He fought for the preservation of Lake
Pedder, which was subsequently lost to
hydro-electric development, but won a battle to
preserve an ancient Huon pine forest on the
banks of the Denison River. At the time of his
death he was assembling photographic
ammunition for a fight to protect the Lower
Gordon River. His life had many achievements,
but it also had a tragic dimension. In 1967 he
lost his house in a bushfire, which destroyed
fifteen years of irreplaceable photographs, and
he lost his own life in the Gordon River in 1972,
drowning in the river he was attempting to save.

Olegas Truchanas (pronounced Tru-har-nas) was born in Siauliai, Lithuania in 1923. During World War II he fought in the Lithuanian Resistance Movement, but fled the country in 1945 with his family to avoid Soviet rule. They reached Munich, where he gained admission to its University to study law, until general unrest forced the building's closure. During this period he climbed in the Bavarian Alps, and his study of Bavarian mountain photography was to influence him for the rest of his life.

He arrived in Tasmania in 1948 as a migrant, and under his visa conditions was required to undertake two years work in industry or public works. He served his two years with the Electrolytic Zinc Company at Risdon near Hobart, where he joined gangs pushing truckloads of metal along an antiquated rail link.

The South-West wilderness region had a reputation for being impenetrable, wild and treacherous, an image that immediately appealed to him. He reasoned that unlike Europe, which had been rigorously explored over the centuries, even aboriginal culture had only peripherally explored the South-West, meaning much of its wild beauty may never have been seen by man.

In 1952 he made the first solo ascent of Federation Peak, a 28 day trek. He was the first to navigate the Serpentine and Lower Gordon rivers, which he accomplished solo, starting the journey from Lake Pedder. His first attempt at this in 1954 was abandoned when he lost his kayak and most of his equipment negotiating a waterfall in the Serpentine gorge. Three years later he was successful, ending the journey at Strahan on Macquarie Harbour. To pass through 'the Splits' (narrow canyons down which the river thundered), he needed to dismantle his canoe and carry it overland to the next accessible point on the river.

His bushwalking ideal was to move through the landscape in anonymity, leaving no trace of his presence through damage or litter, and he tried to instil these values in others.

Truchanas was employed by the Hydro-Electric

Commission, and was dismayed when the State government and his own organisation began to plan a hydro-electric development that would result in the Lake Pedder National Park being flooded under fifty feet of water. He knew the area well, particularly the Lake's quartz beach, two miles long and 600 yards wide, long enough to comfortably use as an airstrip. In his failed effort to halt the development he made a number of audio visual presentations on the threatened area to audiences packed into Hobart's Town Hall.

In February 1967 a bushfire swept through south eastern Tasmania, killing sixty two people and destroying over one and a half thousand properties. His own home went up in flames, incinerating fifteen years of photographs and notes. At a time when he wanted to use his photographs in the fight for Lake Pedder, they lay in ashes. Despite this huge emotional blow, he fought his way back, taking over three thousand photos from that day until his death five years later.

His next battle was successful, as he fought to save a Huon pine forest on the Denison River. Huon pine is found only in Tasmania, and requires between five hundred to one thousand years for a tree to mature. Its exceptional qualities, prized by the timber industry, ensured a vigorous fight, but he prevailed, and the forest received legislative protection.

Truchanas identified the next wilderness threat as the Lower Gordon Power Development Scheme. He knew that his most powerful weapon in the battle would be his photographs, but all his Gordon River photographs had been lost in the 1967 fire, so he set off to replace them. In January 1972 on the Gordon River Truchanas attempted to pull his kayak ashore, but it overturned in the current. Standing on a rock near a waterfall, he tried to pull the canoe into quieter waters, but slipped on the smooth rock and disappeared into the river immediately above the fall. Despite being a strong swimmer, he didn't re-emerge. Peter Dombrovskis, his photographic apprentice, was the first to see his body, thrown against a sunken tree on the river bed.

Dombrovskis went on to continue Truchanas'
work, providing his own photographic
exploration of Tasmania's wilderness regions.

After Truchanas' death his photography exploded
into prominence with the Franklin River protests,
a battle ultimately won by the conservation
movement, which placed environmental issues at
the top of Australia's political agenda for the first
time.

Further reading:
Max Angus, The World of Olegas Truchanas
Australian Conservation Foundation
(first published in 1975, out of print as at
November 2000).

ALSO AVAILABLE FROM ICE CALM:

'What Doesn't Kill Me Makes Me Stronger'

Powerful medicine for overcoming setbacks.

Selected passages from the works of
Friedrich Nietzsche
(1844-1900).

*"I may be a forest and a night of dark trees,
but those not frightened by my darkness
shall discover rosebowers too
beneath my cypresses."*

First published on August 25, 2000
to mark the centenary of Nietzsche's death.

ISBN 0 646 40087 8